The Magic School Bus

PRESENTS
Wild Weather

Scholastic Inc.

Previous page: lightning in the sky

Photos © 2014: Alamy Images: 9 (JLImages), 10 top left (Leon Werdinger), 6 bottom right (RGB Ventures LLC dba SuperStock), 31 bottom left (Ryan McGinnis); Corbis Images: 14 (Hou Jiansen); Getty Images: 4 top left (Anita Stizzoli), 20 top left (Cavan Images), 3 bottom, 25 (Copyright Josh Sommers 2006-2009), 17 (Cultura Science/Jason Persoff Stormdoctor), 6 top left (David Madison), 13 (David Nunuk), 20 bottom right (Gary Pearl), 18 top left (Insight Imaging), 15 top right (Julie Marshall), 1 (Mike Theiss/National Geographic Creative), 28 top left (Panoramic Images), 12 top left (R-J-Seymour), 3 top, 5 (Robert Postma), 19 (Simon Phelps Photography), 26 bottom right (subtik), 3 center, 21 (Wayne R Bilenduke), 29 (Yenwen Lu); iStockphoto: 10 center (Studio-Annika); Mike Hollingshead: cover; NASA: 8 top left (Goddard Space Flight Center Image by Reto Stöckli, enhancements by Robert Simmon), 15 bottom left (Hal Pierce), 26 top left (Image by R.B. Husar, Washington University; the land layer from the SeaWiFS Project; fire maps from the European Space Agency; the sea surface temperature from the Naval Oceanographic Office's Visualization Laboratory; and cloud layer from SSEC, U. of Wisconsin); Nature Picture Library: 20 center (Bryan and Cherry Alexander), 22 top left (David Tipling), 10 bottom right (Grant McDowell), 6 center (Ingo Arndt), 16 top left (Onne van der Wal), 24 top left (Tony Heald); Science Source: 30 (Jim Reed), 31 (Karim Agabi), 16 bottom right (Science Source); Shutterstock, Inc.: 7 (Aleksey Stemmer), 11 (Ensuper), 26 bottom left (Praisaeng), 27 (WDG Photo); Superstock, Inc.: 23 (BlueGreen Pictures).

ISBN 978-0-545-68367-8

Produced by Potomac Global Media, LLC

All text, illustrations, and compilations © 2014 Scholastic Inc.
Based on The Magic School Bus series © Joanna Cole and Bruce Degen
Text by Sean Callery Illustrations by Carolyn Bracken
Consultant: Dr. Pete Inness, meteorology lecturer, University of Reading, England

Published by Scholastic Inc., 557 Broadway, New York, NY 10012.

12 11 10 9 8 7 6 5 4 3 2   14 15 16 17 18 19/0

Cover design by Paul Banks
Interior design by Thomas Keenes
Picture research by Sharon Southren

Printed in the U.S.A.   40
First printing, July 2014

Contents

p. 4

p. 20

p. 24

Weather All Around Us

The rain had almost stopped. Ms. Frizzle pointed to a rainbow in the sky. "The Sun is coming out," she said. The Friz explained that our weather is decided by what happens in Earth's atmosphere. "That's the name we give to all the gases surrounding our planet. Buckle up, and let's take a closer look!"

Rainbow colors appear when the Sun shines through ice crystals in clouds. The effect is called a halo.

Double rainbow

Sometimes raindrops reflect the Sun's light twice. This makes us see a second, fainter rainbow.

Separate colors

The Sun's light is broken down into separate colors. This group of colors is called a spectrum.

Color me a rainbow!

How do rainbows form?

by Wanda

Most rainbows form when the Sun shines on falling raindrops. Light is made up of seven different colors: red, orange, yellow, green, blue, indigo, and violet. When sunlight enters a raindrop, it changes direction and splits up into these different colors. The sunlight passes through lots of raindrops at the same time and we see each of the seven colors as a curved band in the sky.

Frizzle Fact

A rainbow actually makes a perfect circle, but we only ever see the top half as a giant curve, or arc, in the sky.

Up in the Clouds

Clouds are made up of billions of tiny drops of water or ice crystals. They form when water rises up into the air as a gas (water vapor). On reaching cooler air high up, the water turns back into a liquid and may even freeze into crystals.

Lenticular clouds look like spaceships! Their shapes sometimes form when strong winds blow across mountains.

The streaks made by cirrus clouds often have curled ends.

We use the term "overcast" to describe the blanketlike effect of stratus clouds.

Frizzle Fact

Fog is very low cloud cover. It is made up of tiny drops of water that hover near the ground.

Cumulus clouds

These fluffy-looking clouds always have clear outlines.

My head's in the clouds!

Types of clouds
by Arnold

Cumulus clouds are fluffy and white with flat bases. If they stay small and white, it can mean that good weather is on the way. If they start to grow taller and turn gray, that can mean showers and even thunderstorms are on the way. Stratus clouds are flat and look like gray sheets spread low across the sky. They are a sign that drizzle or fog is coming. Cirrus clouds form high up in the sky. They are wispy like hair and can look like streamers. If they start to fill up the sky, it can mean wet weather is on the way.

Low lying

The base of a cumulus cloud may be as low as 1,200 feet (356 meters) from the ground.

Long range

Ribbons of cumulus clouds, often called "streets," can stretch for more than 250 miles (400 kilometers).

There are three main types of clouds: cumulus, stratus, and cirrus clouds.

Water Everywhere

Earth is sometimes called the Blue Planet. This is because the oceans that cover about 70 percent of the Earth look blue from space. This water has always been on the planet, constantly changing from liquid to gas or ice as it moves between the ground and the air. We call this the water cycle.

This is our planet. The liquid water looks blue from space. The wispy white shapes are clouds. The solid white area at the top of the picture is ice.

Water as a liquid
The most common form of water on planet Earth is liquid. This is the type that flows in rivers and oceans.

Water as a gas

Usually, we cannot see water vapor rising into the sky. When it cools to form droplets, however, we see it as clouds.

Water gets around!

Water as a solid

When water freezes, it becomes hard and solid. Ice and snow are common forms of frozen water.

The water cycle
by Keesha

When heat from the Sun warms the water in oceans, some of it turns into vapor. This rises until it cools into droplets, which form clouds. The droplets join up to make bigger drops, which fall as rain. Some of the water falls in rivers and flows toward the sea, where the cycle starts again.

condensation

precipitation

evaporation

Frizzle Fact

Thanks to the water cycle, a glass of water could contain tiny parts from drops that washed an Egyptian queen in the distant past.

Rain!

Water falls to Earth as rain. It fills lakes, ponds, rivers, and streams and helps plants to grow. We could not live without drinking freshwater. Seawater is too salty for us to drink. Too much rainfall can cause flooding.

Deserts are mostly hot and dry but they do get rain, sometimes in short, heavy bursts that can cause flash floods.

Frogs can live on land and in water so they don't mind at all when it rains!

Rainfall has flooded this farmland. Floods happen when water cannot drain away fast enough.

Frizzle Fact

One of the wettest places on Earth is Mount Waialeale in Hawaii, which gets more than 423 inches (1,074 centimeters) of rain a year.

Some rain that falls during a storm soaks into the soil.

Too much rain can cause mudslides that destroy roads and houses.

Water, water everywhere!

Splish, splash!

What are monsoons?
by Ralphie

Monsoons are strong winds that bring heavy rain with them. They can happen in Asia, Africa, Australia, and on the Pacific coast of Central America. It can pour with rain for weeks at a time. Monsoons can be important for the people who live in some of these regions, because the rain brings them water to drink and helps their crops to grow. So, although monsoons can also bring floods, people rely on them for their survival.

Wind Power

Wind is just air on the move. Its movement is caused by changes in the temperature of air, land, and water. When hot air rises, cold air flows in to fill the space left behind, and this makes wind. Wind can move slowly to make a breeze, or it can move very quickly in a gale.

A jet stream is a current of air that flows super fast, high in the sky. It is so strong that it speeds up an airplane flying with it.

Look how fast the windmills are spinning!

We can't see the wind, but we can feel it. Trees sway, and dust, rain, and snow are blown around by wind.

Wind farm

A collection of windmills is called a wind farm. Some wind farms are built on land, while others are built at sea.

It's nitty-gritty!

What are sandstorms?
by Dorothy Ann

Sandstorms happen in the desert and other very dry areas. They occur when powerful winds lift millions of grains of sand or dust in the air and carry them off — sometimes tens of thousands of miles (thousands of kilometers) away. Some sandstorms can last for several days. About 1 billion tons (900 million tonnes) of dust blow out of northern Africa every year.

Rotating blades

The wind turns the blades of this windmill. As the blades rotate, they turn an engine to make electricity.

Frizzle Fact

The windiest place on Earth is Port Martin in Antarctica. The wind blows at more than 40 miles (64 kilometers) per hour on at least one hundred days of the year.

Hurricane!

Hurricanes are called typhoons in the Pacific and cyclones in India, but all three terms mean the same thing.

Fierce winds
Hurricane winds are so strong that they can rip trees from the ground.

Frizzle Fact
A storm becomes a hurricane if the wind blows faster than 74 miles (119 kilometers) per hour. That's the speed of a sprinting cheetah.

Hurricanes are storms with strong winds and heavy rain. They start over the warm waters near the equator and happen when hot water vapor rises to form clouds. The clouds and wind start to spin and form a storm that rushes toward land. Once on land, hurricanes can cause great damage.

Hurricanes can create waves that are 20 feet (6 meters) higher than normal waves.

Hurricane Patterns

Spiral form

A hurricane forms a circle of clouds as wide as 340 miles (550 kilometers) across. That's as big as the state of Texas.

We don't use the letters Q, U, X, Y, or Z.

The eye

The storm swirls around a calm, still center, called the "eye."

Wind direction

Hurricanes in the Northern Hemisphere spin counterclockwise. In the Southern Hemisphere they spin in a clockwise direction.

How do you name a hurricane?
by Wanda

The Atlantic hurricane season is from June to November. Every year, each new hurricane is given a boy's or girl's name beginning with a different letter of the alphabet, starting from A. So the first hurricane of the year might be called Arnold, the second Beth, the third Charlie, and so on. There are six lists of names to choose from, and they are rotated annually. But the names of big storms — like Hurricane Katrina (2005) and Hurricane Sandy (2012) — are retired and never used again.

Tornado!

A tornado is a fast-spinning tube of air that links the ground to a cloud in the sky. They develop during some thunderstorms and are also called twisters. Tornado winds are the strongest on Earth, reaching 300 miles (500 kilometers) per hour. They are strong enough to lift cows, cars, and even houses high into the air.

Cumulonimbus clouds like these are tall, dark, and dense clouds that form when strong air currents carry water vapor upward. They are also called thunderclouds. Some cumulonimbus clouds can produce tornadoes.

Waterspouts

Tornadoes at sea
A tornado that forms over seas or lakes is called a waterspout.

Spinning cloud
A waterspout is really just a fast-spinning cloud.

Water-free
A waterspout does not suck up water as it moves, although it looks as though that's what it is doing.

Frizzle Fact
In 1931, a twister in Minnesota carried a railroad car 80 feet (24 meters) from the track with 117 passengers on board. The car weighed 83 tons (75 tonnes)!

Stormy clouds
Twisters link with dark, heavy, cumulonimbus thunderclouds.

A storm's brewing!

What is Tornado Alley?
by Phoebe

While tornadoes can happen anywhere, the United States has the most. Around 1,200 tornadoes a year spin through Tornado Alley in the Midwest. This is because hot air moving north from the Gulf of Mexico meets cold polar winds coming south. Enormous thunderclouds form when the hot and cold air clashes.

MT ND MN
WY SD
CO NE IA
KS MO IL IN OH
OK AR TN KY
TX MS
LA ········ Tornado Alley

Funnel cloud
The column of a tornado is called a funnel cloud. You can see it because it is full of tiny drops of water.

Destructive force
Tornadoes can do a lot of damage, especially to cars and mobile homes.

Most tornadoes last just a few minutes and travel around 4 miles (6.5 kilometers). It would take most adults at least an hour to walk that far.

17

Thunder and Lightning

Lightning rods protect skyscrapers and other tall buildings. They work by conducting the electricity to the ground safely.

Lightning happens in a storm, when ice in the clouds becomes charged with electricity and causes a giant spark. Thunder is the sound of air expanding from the heat in the lightning. We hear it after seeing the lightning flash because light travels faster than sound.

Lightning clouds
Lightning is usually made by cumulonimbus clouds that are very tall and full of water and ice.

Speedy strike
Lightning travels at up to 136,000 miles (219,000 kilometers) per hour.

Frizzle Fact
Lightning heats the air to around 54,000 degrees Fahrenheit (30,000 degrees Celsius). That's five times hotter than the surface of the Sun.

Sheet lightning
Lightning flashes that occur inside a cloud are called sheet lightning.

Quick as a flash!

Storm safety
by Carlos

Lightning kills around fifty people a year in the United States. People get hit because they are mainly made of water, and water conducts electricity. The best way to avoid being struck by lightning is to stay inside a building or vehicle during a thunderstorm. If you are outside, avoid open areas, water, and tall objects like trees and poles. Don't hold an umbrella or fly a kite. Crouch low, but don't lie down. Inside, don't use a corded phone because electricity can travel along the wires.

Forked lightning
Forked is the term given to lightning that forms branches as it travels from the cloud to the ground.

Snowstorms

Snow is made up of tiny ice crystals. The crystals form when drops of water freeze in very cold temperatures. Snow is mostly air, which is why snowflakes are bigger than raindrops but take longer to fall. A snowflake can take up to an hour to float to the ground.

This is what a snowflake looks like under a microscope. Every snowflake is unique, but most have six points.

Arctic dogs have very thick coats to protect them from freezing in the cold and snow.

Snowplows clear roads and push big drifts of snow out of the way.

Frizzle Fact

The worst blizzard in US history happened in March 1888. Some 50 inches (127 centimeters) of snow fell in just 36 hours in Connecticut.

Polar bears

Polar bears live near the North Pole and have thick fur to keep out the cold. They don't slip because they have long curved claws to grip the ice.

Stay calm!

A blizzard is a kind of snowstorm. Wind speeds can reach 45 miles (72 kilometers) per hour.

What is a whiteout?
by Tim

A whiteout is a dangerous type of blizzard. This is when there is so much snow blowing around in the air that people cannot see farther than a few feet (meters) around them. They may not know where they are anymore and can get lost very quickly. People in cars are advised to stop moving. It is also hard to tell the land and the sky apart. Flying in these conditions is dangerous because pilots cannot see the ground.

Polar lands

It is never warm enough for the ice to thaw near the North Pole. The landscape is always white there.

Freezing Weather

The parts of the world that are farthest north and south get less sun. This means they are colder. The coldest continent is Antarctica, home to the South Pole. Temperatures there never rise above freezing.

Antarctica is cold and windy, but it is also dry because it hardly ever rains. That means it can also be called a desert!

Emperor penguin chicks huddle together to keep warm on the Antarctic ice.

Floating ice

Icebergs are huge chunks of floating ice, sometimes as large as a ten-story building. Around 90 percent of an iceberg is underwater.

Frizzle Fact

The Earth's lowest-ever temperature was recorded in Antarctica, on July 21, 1983. It was a chilly 128.6 degrees below zero Fahrenheit (minus 89.2 degrees Celsius).

Higher means colder

The higher the elevation, the lower the temperature will be. It drops by about 3.5 degrees Fahrenheit (2 degrees Celsius) for every 1,000-foot (305-meter) rise in altitude.

I'm f-f-f-freezing!

An ice age is when the temperature on Earth drops and ice covers the land. There have been lots of ice ages in Earth's life. The last one ended ten thousand years ago.

A long way down

Almost all of Antarctica is made of ice that is around 1 mile (1.6 kilometers) thick. That's deeper than any skyscraper is tall.

Life in Antarctica
by Arnold

No one lives in Antarctica, but scientists go there to do research, sometimes staying for many weeks. Life there is tough. People have to wear lots of layers of clothes to stay warm. The outer layer needs to be able to keep out the wind and snow. It is hard to get freshwater, so people use as little as possible and always wash quickly in the shower. They grow some food for themselves, in greenhouses, but most of what they eat is shipped in.

Turquoise glow

The bright blue appearance of this water is caused by daylight reflecting off ice just below the surface.

Hot Weather

A heat wave is when the weather is very, very hot for days on end. If it goes on for months and there is no rain, it can lead to a drought. The land dries up and the soil cracks and is blown away. Crops die, which can mean there is not enough food for people to eat.

When it is very hot, the air bends the light. It plays tricks on our eyes. These zebras look as if they are standing in water.

Our heat comes from the Sun.

LET'S BLOW!

The city of Yuma, Arizona, has around 4,300 hours of sunshine a year. This makes it the sunniest place in the world.

Frizzle Fact

The hottest place on Earth is Dallol, Ethiopia. The average temperature is 93 degrees Fahrenheit (34 degrees Celsius).

Cloudless skies
With so little water in the air, no clouds can form and it will not rain.

Dried earth
The ground becomes so dry during a drought that it cracks open. Nothing can grow here.

Hot stuff!

How hot is hot?
by Keesha

A record-breaking heat wave spread across much of Europe in August 2003. The highest temperature was recorded in Portugal. It was 117 degrees Fahrenheit (47 degrees Celsius). Roads melted, train tracks twisted, and lakes and rivers dried up. Many people died because their bodies could not cope with the extreme heat.

Weather Forecasting

The weather changes all the time. Forecasters try to predict our weather hours, days, and even weeks in advance. They look at the weather in different parts of the world to help them decide what will happen next. They also look for patterns in weather records from the past.

This picture shows Earth's ocean temperatures. Blue areas are cold, red are hot. The large red area shows warm water in the Pacific Ocean.

A weather vane turns according to which way the wind is blowing.

Weather Station

Wind speed and direction
This instrument measures the speed and direction of the wind. The information helps decide how the weather will change in the next few hours.

Countrywide forecasts
A weather station collects information on what the weather is like in one place. Using several of them helps forecasters see how the weather is changing across the country.

Solar energy
This solar panel gets energy from the Sun. The energy powers the equipment, allowing the weather station to send information to the forecaster.

Rain, rain, go away!

Forecasters get their information from all kinds of places: weather stations on land, ships and floating weather buoys at sea, balloons floating high in the sky, and satellites watching from space.

Can humans make the weather change?
by Ralphie

It is possible for humans to change the weather for short periods of time. One method for doing this is called cloud seeding. Chemicals are placed in rockets and fired into clouds or released from airplanes. The chemicals make the cloud more likely to release rain. This helps farmers in need of water for their crops. The same method has also been used at major sporting events to prevent crowds from getting soaked.

Frizzle Fact

The highest weather station on land is on Mount Everest, the world's tallest mountain. Unmanned, it records the weather 26,000 feet (7,925 meters) up!

Changing Climate

Factories developed from the 1800s onward. They introduced the use of fuels such as coal and oil.

This is Los Angeles, where smog often makes the air look gray and hazy. The city gets a lot of smog because it is built in a big valley, where the air doesn't move very much.

When the bus flew back over the city, Phoebe said the air looked foggy. Ms. Frizzle told us this was smog — pollution that hangs in the air. "There are also gases that we can't see," she said. She explained that these were greenhouse gases and that they were making the planet hotter. "We call it global warming — and it may bring more wild weather in the future."

The sea level and sea temperatures are slowly rising. This changes weather patterns, making it more likely for coastlines to flood.

Traffic pollution
A lot of smog comes from gases produced by cars and trucks as they travel along city freeways.

How can we help the planet?
by Dorothy Ann

I'm going green!

Here are some ways we can help the planet stay healthy:
- Use less energy by switching off lights you don't need.
- Help plant trees to absorb carbon dioxide from the air.
- Save water — take a shower rather than a bath.
- Recycle your waste.
- Whenever possible, walk or ride a bicycle instead of using the car.

Greenhouse gases
Carbon dioxide and some other gases are called greenhouse gases. They trap heat, just like the glass sides of a greenhouse keep in the warmth from the Sun.

Frizzle Fact
Earth's average temperature has risen 1.4 degrees Fahrenheit (0.8 degrees Celsius) since 1880, when we started burning lots of coal and oil. The decade 2000 to 2009 was the warmest ever recorded.

Weather Professionals

Many jobs have something to do with measuring and studying the weather. Some people forecast what the weather is likely to do next. Others chase storms to watch and record the effects that weather has on the world around us.

Storm chasers

Storm chasers track all sorts of extreme weather. For example, they wait for warnings about tornadoes, and while almost everybody else stays indoors, they head to where the storm may pass. They follow a storm to record what happens.

Meteorologists

Meteorologists are scientists who study changes in the weather. They gather information such as the amount of rainfall, wind speed and direction, and temperature in a region. Then they use the information to help predict the weather.

Weather forecasters

These meteorologists say what the weather will be like in the future in a certain area. They gather information on meteorological measurements from satellites and weather balloons. They look at where clouds are and how the wind is blowing. Using this data, they can give accurate forecasts for days and sometimes even a month to come.

Climatologists

These meteorologists study the Earth's climate (its long-term weather patterns). They do so by looking at data collected over months and years. The information they give us can tell us about what kinds of plants and animals survive in different parts of the world.

Atmospheric science teachers

An atmospheric science teacher trains people to study the Earth's atmosphere — the bubble of gases that separates us from space. They help students to understand the power of nature, how to predict storms, and why climate change happens.

Words to Know

Altitude The height of something above the ground or above sea level.

Atmosphere The mixture of gases that surrounds planet Earth.

Climate The weather that is typical of a place over a long period of time.

Climate change Global warming and other changes in the weather and weather patterns that are happening because of human activity.

Current The movement of air in a definite direction.

Desert A dry area where hardly any plants grow because there is so little rain.

Drought A long period without rain.

Flood To overflow with water beyond normal limits.

Global warming A gradual rise in the temperature of Earth's atmosphere, caused by human activities that pollute.

Hemisphere One half of a round object, especially of the Earth.

Polar Near or having to do with the icy regions around the North or South Pole.

Satellite A spacecraft that is sent into orbit around the Earth, the Moon, or another heavenly body. Weather satellites watch and record the Earth's weather.

Sea level The average level of the ocean's surface, used as a starting point from which to measure the height or depth of a place.

Spectrum The bands of color that are revealed when light shines through drops of water, as in a rainbow.

Water vapor The gas that water turns into when it is heated by the Sun.